CHINESE

WRITING PRACTICE BOOK

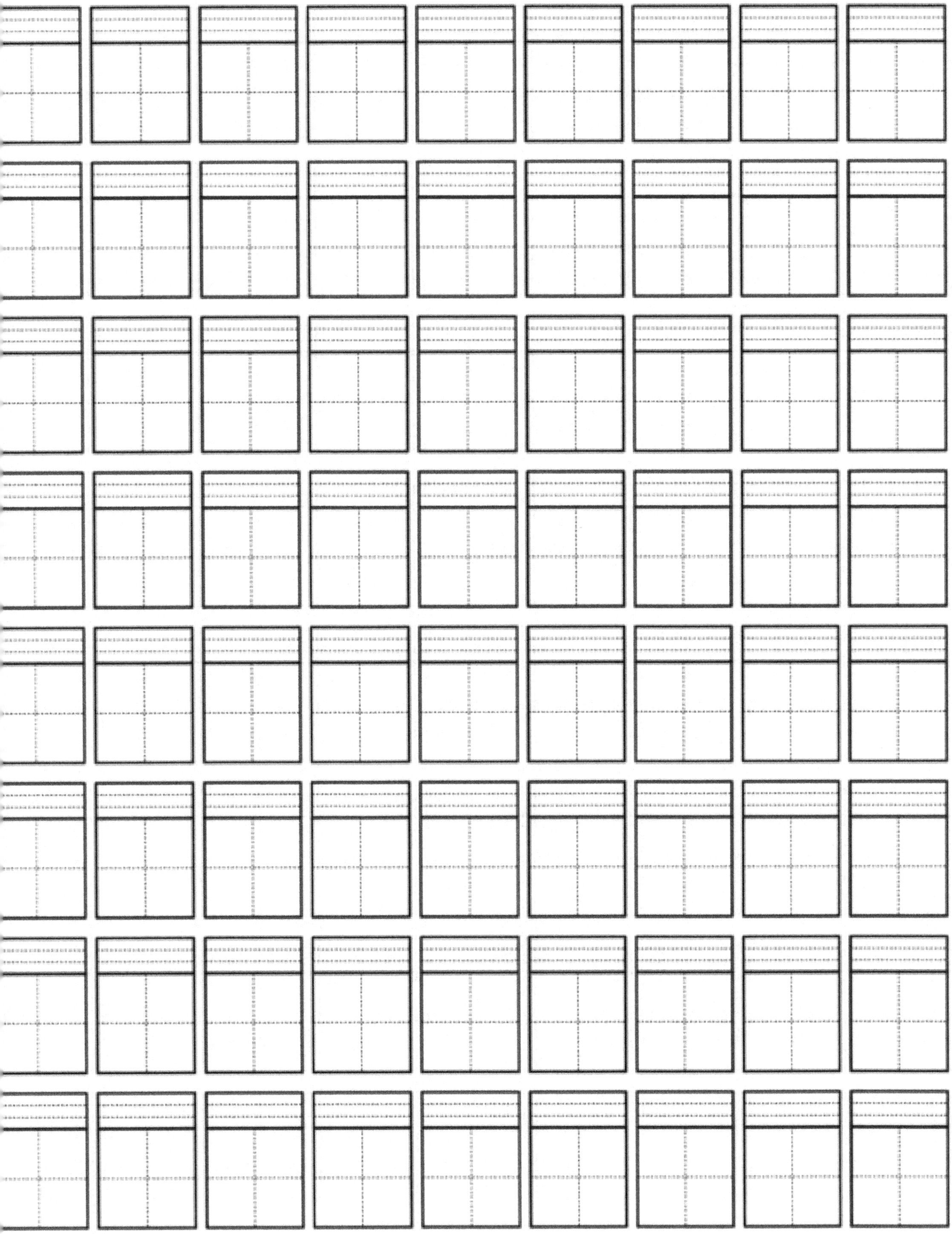

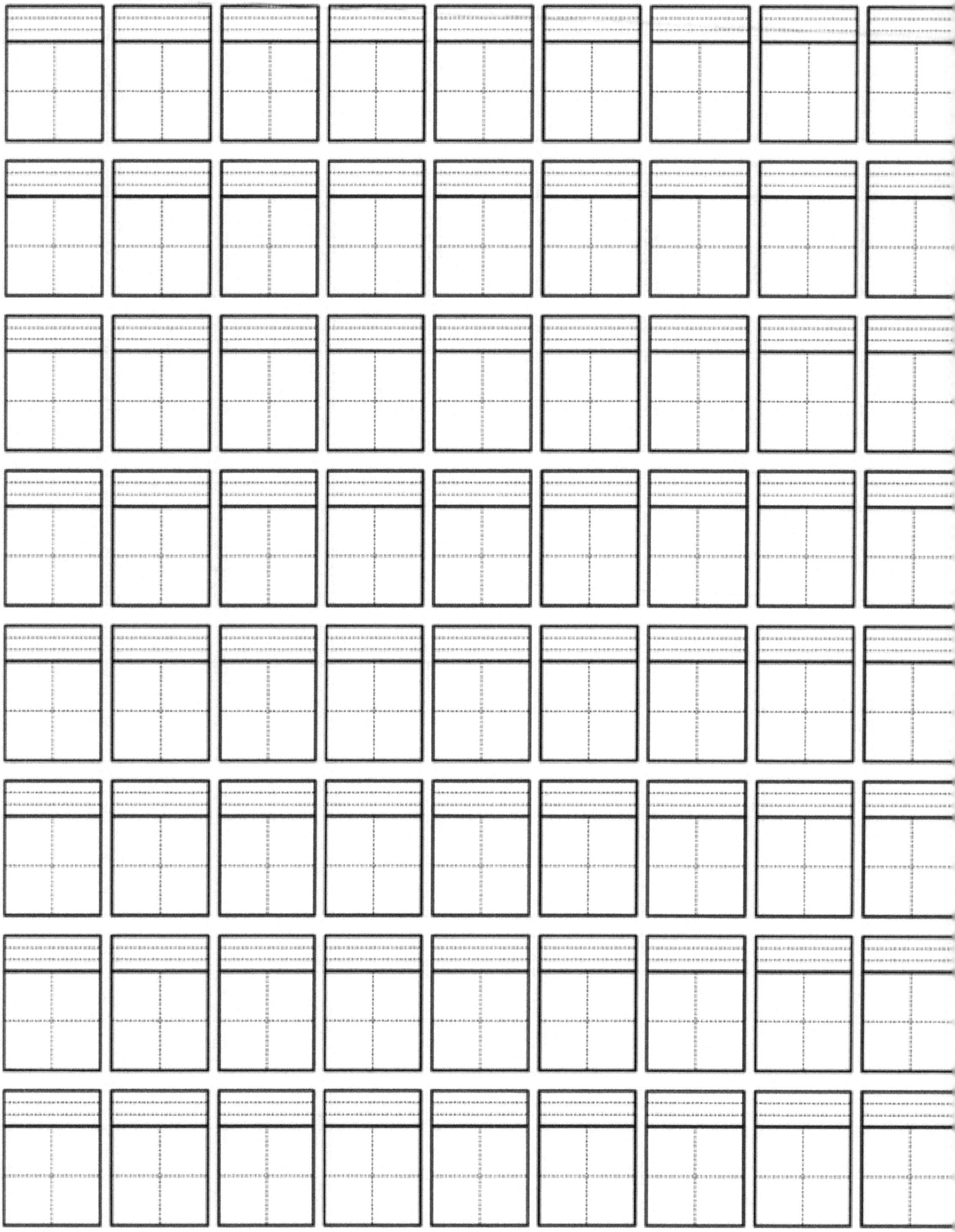

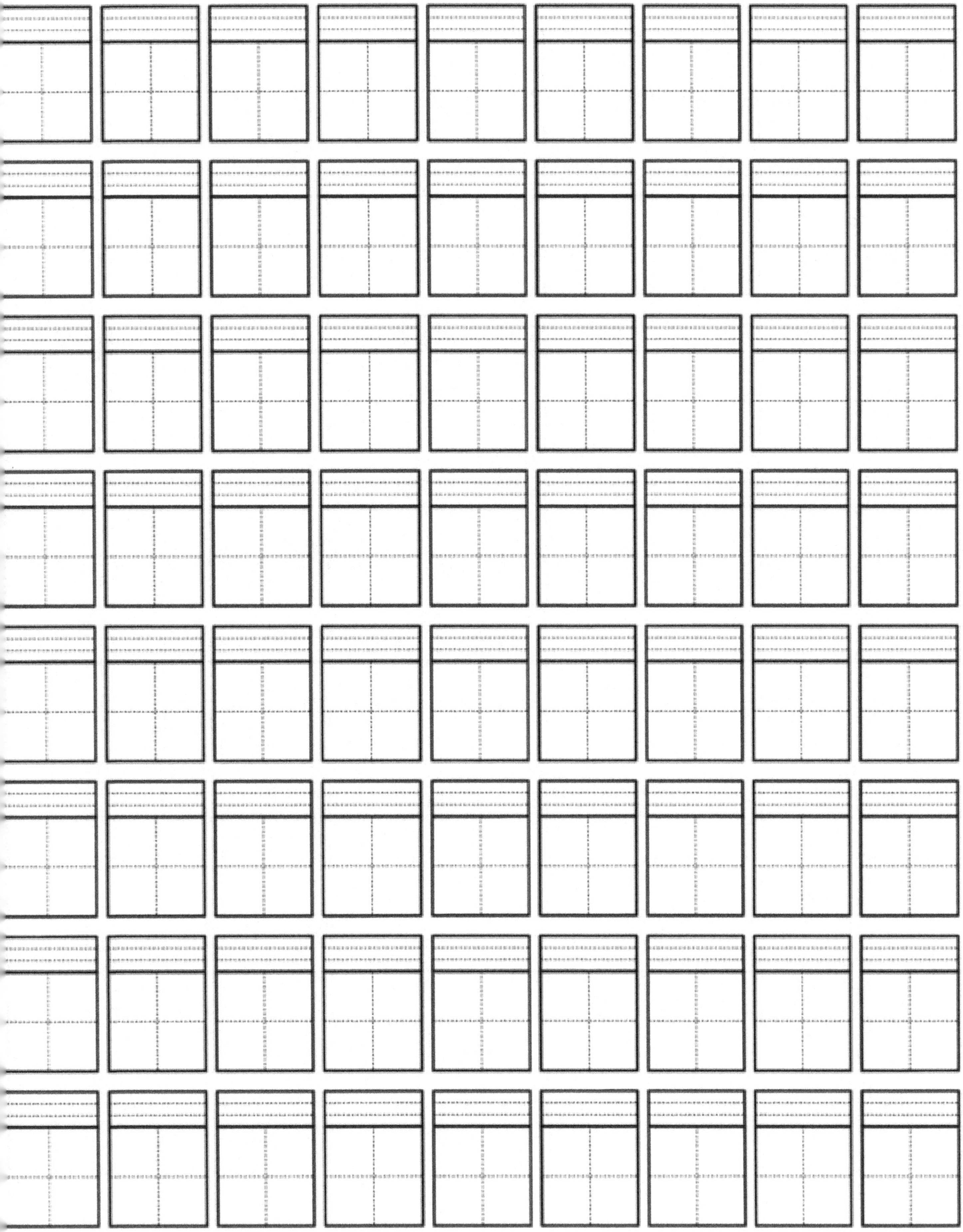

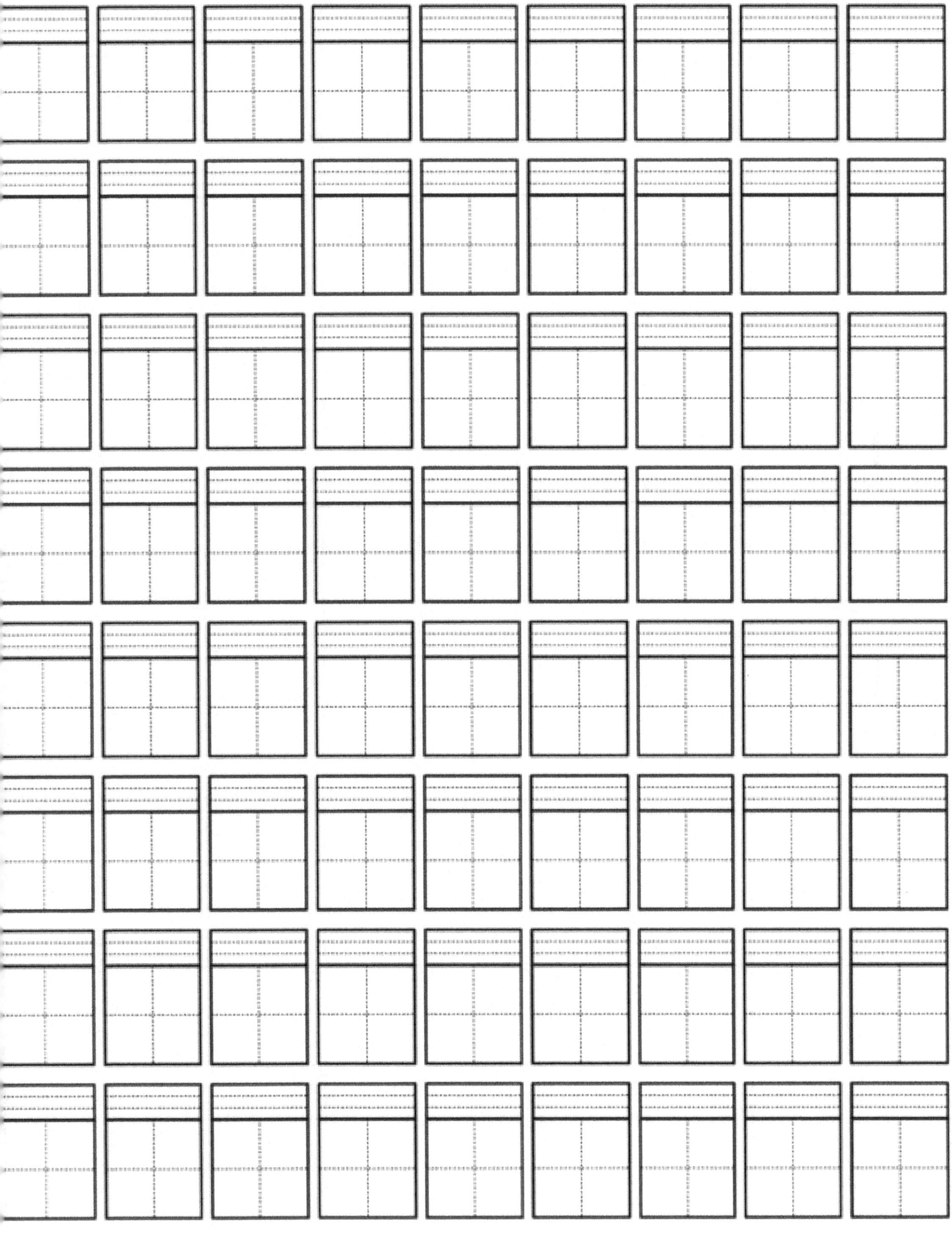

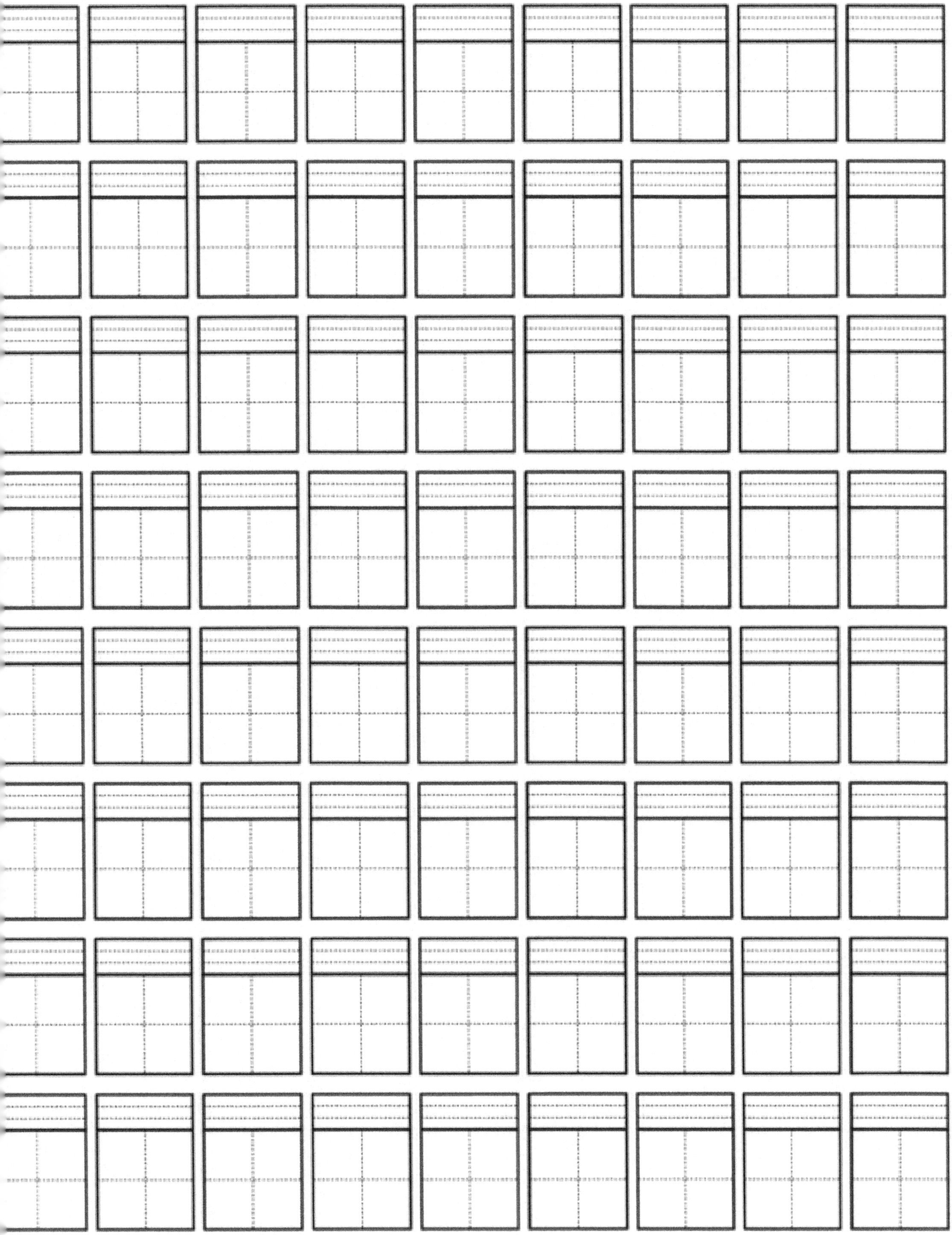

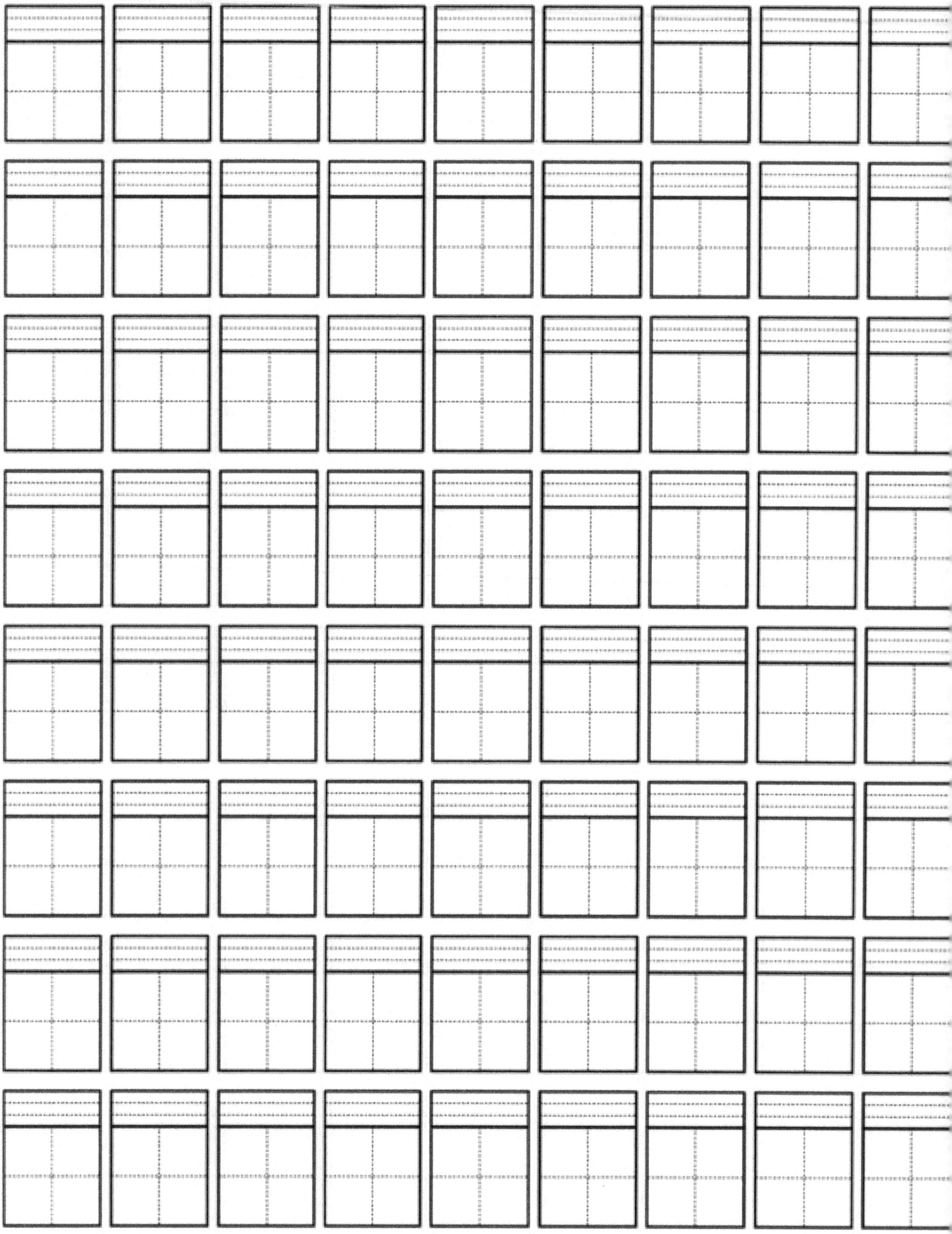

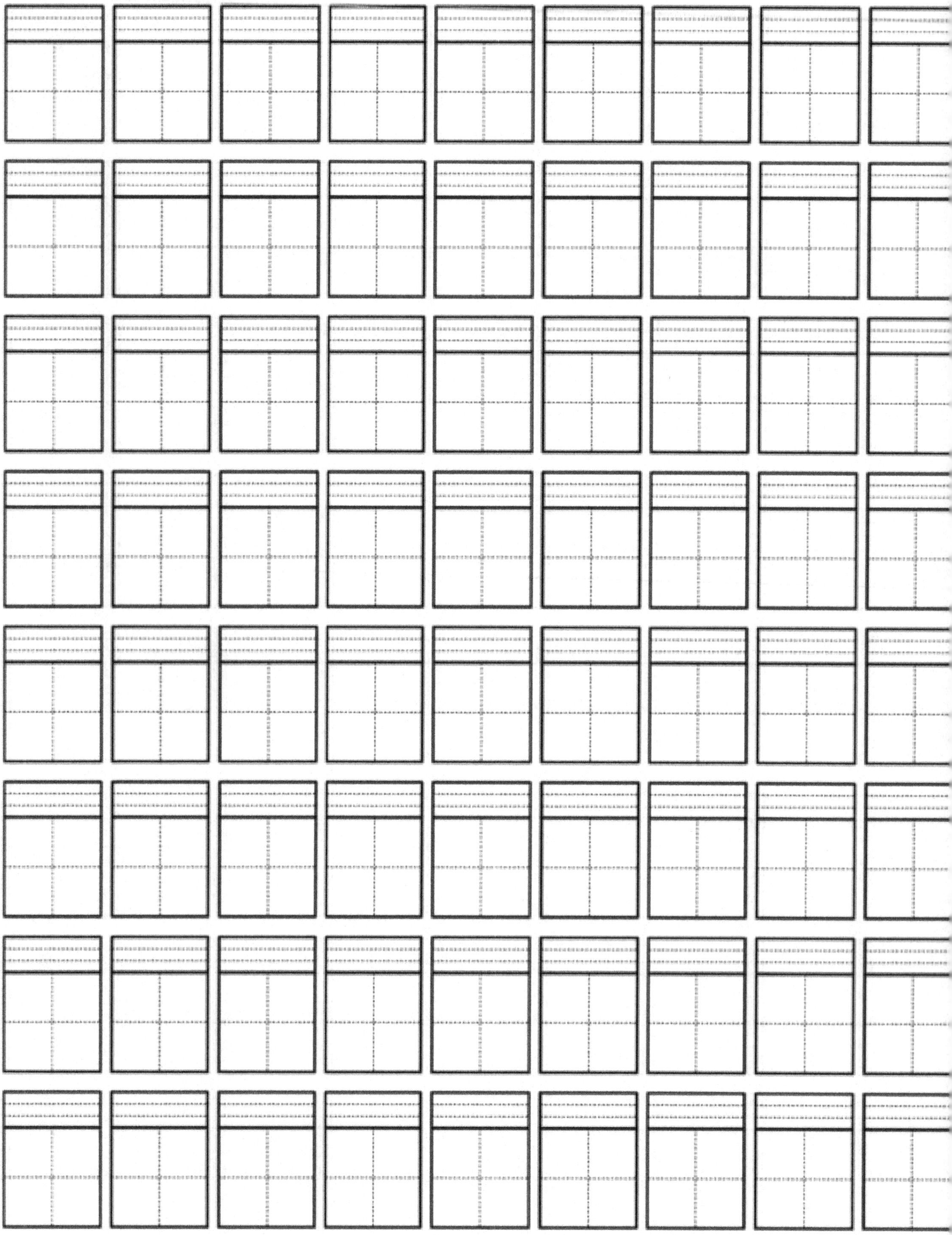

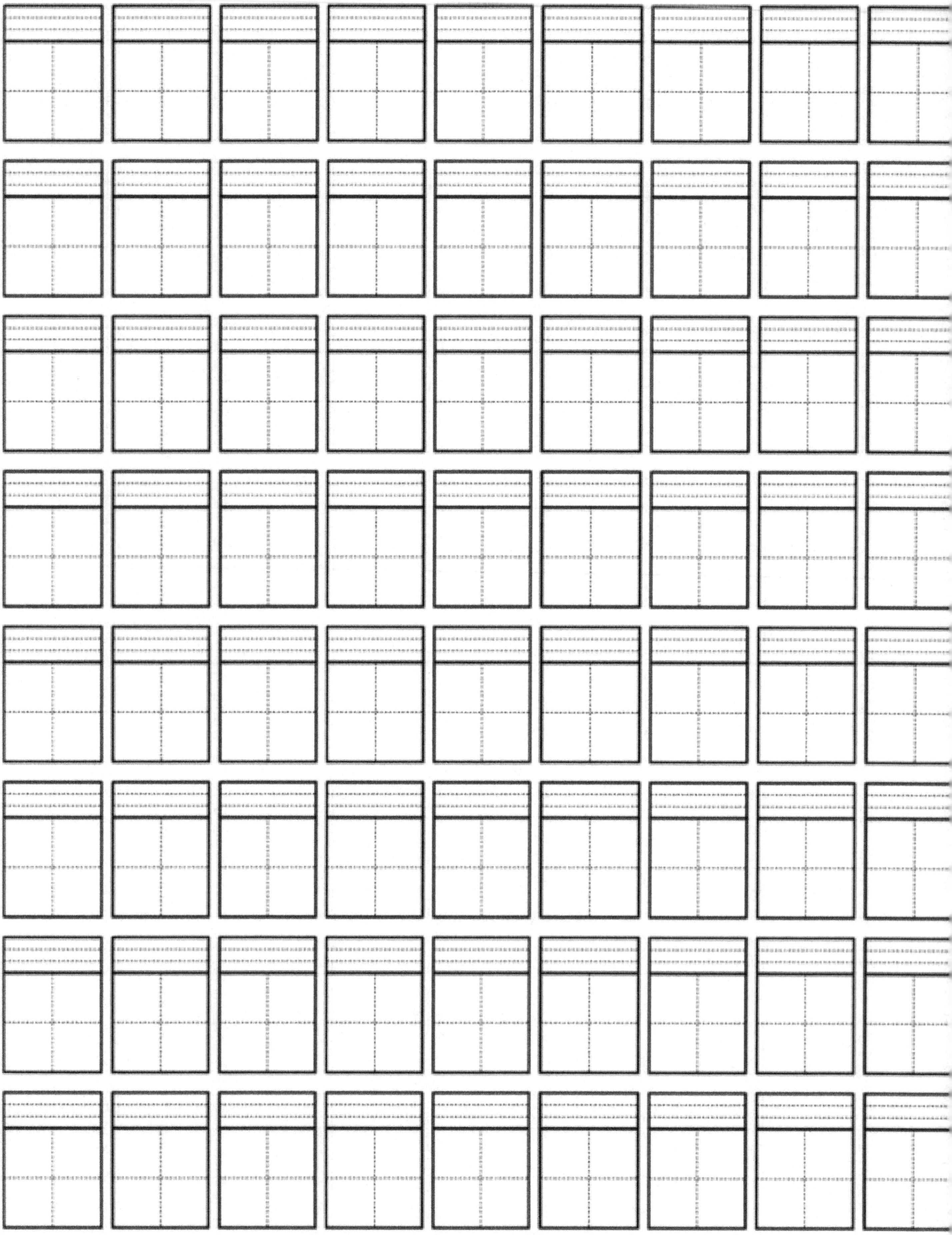

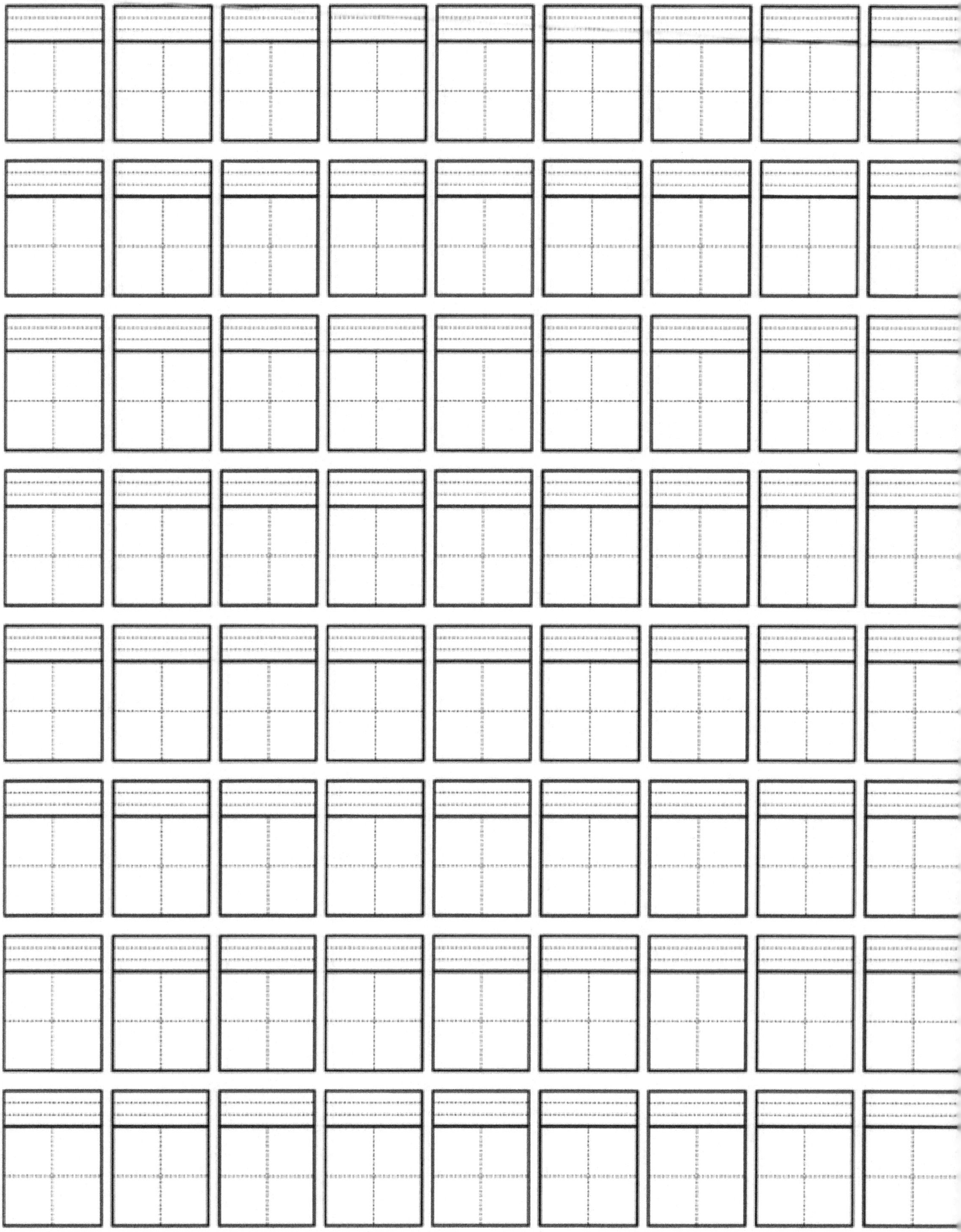

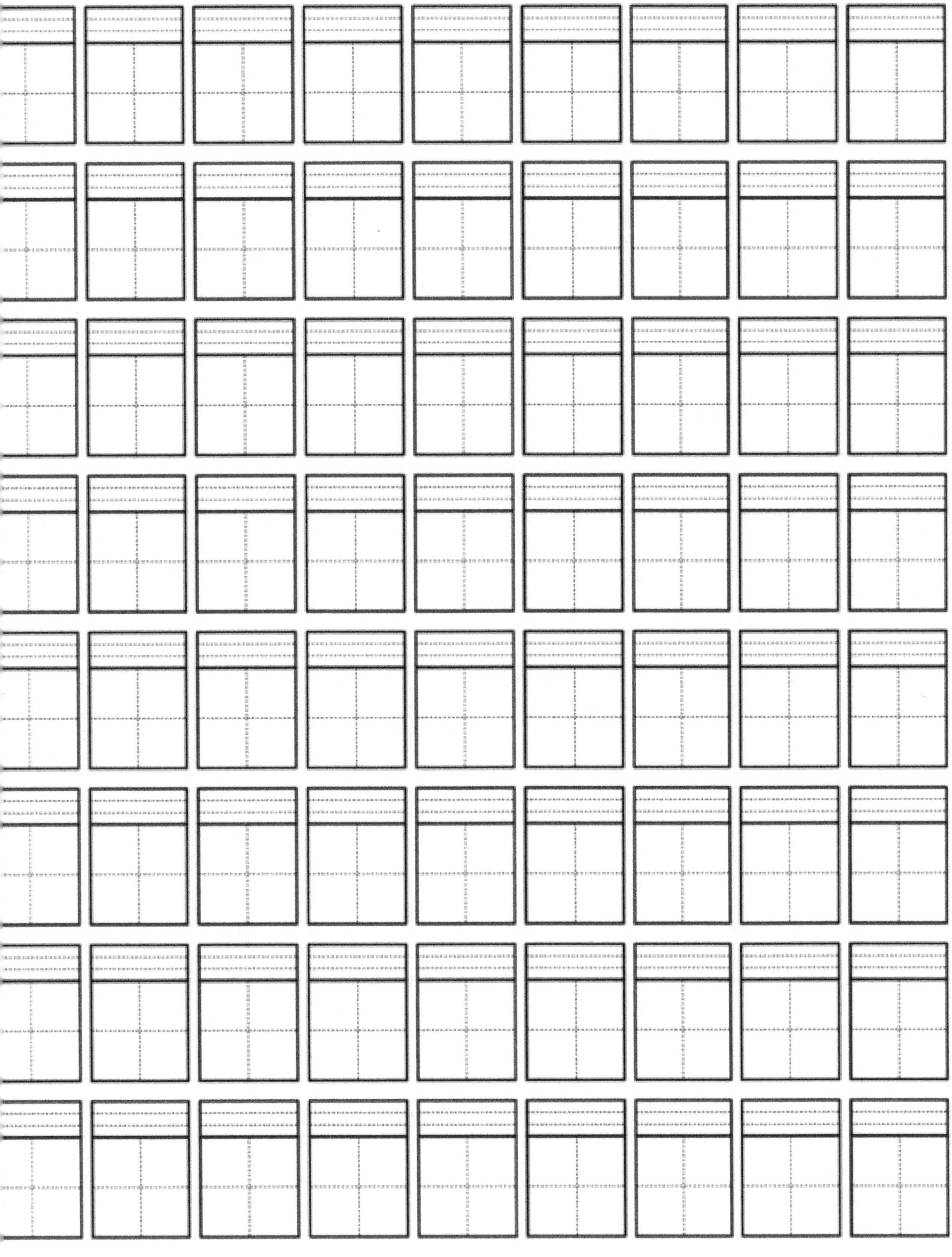

Made in the USA
Las Vegas, NV
23 February 2021

18455090R00057